CW00427859

Contents

Introduction

As a driving instructor, a question I get asked by a lot of my learners is:

'What kind of things can you fail for on a driving test?'

To answer this question would take a very long time as there are a lot of things you can fail for. To make it easier, I have listed the top 100 ways that people fail for. Knowing what to look out for and what to avoid during your test will give you an advantage. By reading and understanding these faults you will get a better understanding of what the examiners are looking out for as you do your test.

Knowing what faults to look out for is half the battle. Wouldn't you like to know how to avoid them in the first place? Each of the faults listed has several ways of avoiding it.

Beginning of test

So you have made it this far. After hours of lessons, getting through the theory test, you have finally got to the day you take your driving test. There are some things to remember before you go to the test centre to start you on the right path.

 I have listed some obstacles that may trip you up before you even begin your test:

1. Arriving late

Yes this seems obvious but you will be surprised how many people turn up late for their driving test. The examiners usually give a few minutes grace but if you are more than 10 minutes the test will be cancelled.

How to avoid this:

- *Plan your journey so you arrive nice and early.*
- *Make sure you know how to get to the test centre.*
- *Check the time of your test the day before so you know exactly when you have to be there.*

2. Arriving at the wrong test centre

With a lot of test centres being near each other, it can be easy sometimes to get mixed up and go to the wrong one. If you are at the wrong one and you realise too late you may not be able to get to the correct one on time.

How to avoid this:

- *Check your email confirmation for the test centre before going there.*

- *Check the name of the road as some test centres have the same name but different locations.*
- *Check again when you are waiting for the examiners.*

3. Forgetting your driving licence

Sounds silly, but yes it does happen. The driving test cannot go ahead if you can't show the examiner your provisional licence.

How to avoid this:

- *keep your licence in a safe place in the days leading to the driving test*
- *check that you have it before leaving your house*
- *bring it with you when you go into the waiting area, don't leave it in your car.*

4. Not having a car

You read that right, not having a car. A few test candidates have turned up to test centres thinking that the DVSA will provide the test vehicle. If you are not going with an instructor, you must go with someone else and have the correct insurance for you to drive that car on a test.

How to avoid this:

- *go with a driving instructor*
- *if you have to use your own car make sure it is in good condition and fit for the road.*

5. Bringing an unsuitable car

If you bring your own car. Make sure that it is road worthy as problems such as a broken brake light will mean that you will not be able to use that car for the test.

How to avoid this:

- *Take a driving instructor's car. They know what is expected in terms of the condition of the car*
- *check all your bulbs before going to the test*
- *check your tyres are safe and legal*
- *have suitable L-Plates*
- *have spare bulbs. If there is a problem with your bulbs you will get a little bit of time to fix it*
- *make sure you know how to replace any bulbs or tyres. If you are given the chance to fix the problem it would be better if you know how to fix it so you can do it quickly*
- *check tyres for nails before going into the waiting area, noticing this early may give you enough time to change the tyre.*

6. Failing eye test

Before going into the car to begin the test, you will be asked to read some number plates from 27.5m away. If you cannot do this, the test will not go ahead and a fail will be recorded.

How to prevent this:

- *test your eyes before starting lessons*
- *if you feel your eye sight is not all there, go to the opticians*
- *don't forget your glasses if you wear them.*

If you have managed to avoid all of the above, you are off to a good start. Now relax, and settle into the test. It may take a few minutes for the nerves to settle but once you get into it, you will be much calmer than you think. There are some more pointers for you to think about as you carry on your test.

Moving off and stopping

As you go about your test, there will be a lot of moving off and stopping. Some of it will just be normal moving off and stopping at lights or in traffic. Other times you will be asked to pull over and then move off again. This has the potential for a few mistakes:

7. Allowing the car to roll back too far

Hill starts are not much fun for a lot of drivers. They can be terrifying for some. Add another vehicle that has stopped too closely behind into the mixture and the stress can be overwhelming. It doesn't have to be though.

The car rolling back can be the result of several scenarios:

- loss of control of the pedals
- handbrake not applied high enough
- stalling then letting the car roll back
- not enough of a biting point before releasing the handbrake
- not paying attention and failing to notice that the car is rolling back.

Allowing the car to roll back won't mean that you fail straight away. If you let the car roll back too far, the examiner will have to intervene and that is when you will fail the test. The examiner will intervene sooner if there is another vehicle close behind.

How to avoid this fault:

- *Apply handbrake properly – a half applied handbrake won't hold the car on steep hills. Take your foot off the brake to make sure that the handbrake is holding the car still. If it is not then pull it up higher*

- *Use brakes if you are rolling back – a common mistake is to try and use the handbrake to stop the car once it starts rolling downhill. This will not be as effective as using the footbrake. The handbrake should only be used after you have stopped the car with your footbrake*
- *Take your time before moving off*
- *Make sure you have a strong enough biting point before releasing the handbrake*
- *Use enough gas – having just the biting won't always work on very steep hills. Use the gas to give the car the push it needs to get up the hill*
- *Control the clutch – once you have enough gas and you are at the biting point, make sure you don't lose the biting point by pressing down on the clutch unnecessarily or releasing the clutch too soon*
- *If you stall, use the brake straight away to control the car, apply the handbrake, take a breath, relax and try again*
- *The main thing is to keep calm*

8. Signalling too early when pulling over

Signals tell other road users what you intend to do. When pulling over, be sure that you do not have your left signal on as you go past a road on your left. Can you think what might happen if another car was waiting to come out of that road and they see you signal left as you approach the junction?

How to avoid this fault:

- *identify where you are going to pull over before signalling*
- *if there are roads by where you want to pull over, wait until you have gone past that road before signalling left*
- *if you realise early enough, you can cancel your signal (be careful as once people have seen your signal they may have already made up their mind about what you are doing and may be checking elsewhere so proceed with caution).*

9. Stopping too suddenly

When you are pulling over, other drivers need time to react to this and plan their way around you. If you pull over too suddenly with not much warning to the vehicle behind you, could you think of what might happen? How might it affect the driver behind you?

How to avoid this fault:

- *identify where you want to pull over first*
- *signal nice and early (taking into account the point above)*
- *slow down gradually*
- *avoid braking harshly*
- *check your mirrors to see who is around you.*

10. **Stopping in front of a driveway**

During the test, you will be asked to pull over several times. The examiner will say something along the lines of:

'Pull over on the left, on this occasion you can ignore any driveways.'

If you hear this then it is fine to block a driveway on that one occasion. It is not a trick as some people might like to think.

The examiner might also say something like:

'Pull over on the left in a safe place.'

This means that it's down to you to identify a safe place, signal and pull over. Do not block a drive way as this may obstruct people from accessing their driveways. Blocking a driveway will get you a minor fault. However, if a driver wants to use that driveway to drive in or out and they can't because you are in the way, this will be a serious fault. You might think 'What are the chances of that happening?' More than you think!

How to avoid this fault:

- *before signalling, identify where you are going to pull over*
- *aim for parking bays if they are there*
- *aim for long raised curbs rather than really short ones*
- *if you realise you have stopped in front of a driveway, drive forward or reverse a bit to where you are not causing a blockage (do this safely and let the examiner know what you are doing).*

11. **Driving onto the pavement as you pull over**

Slightly making contract with the curb will not usually be enough to fail the test. If you mount the pavement then this is a different story altogether. What might be the consequences of mounting the pavement?

How to avoid this fault:

- *reduce your speed so that by the time you are near the pavement you are going very slowly*
- *use a reference point, for most people it is when the curb looks like it is roughly in the centre of your windscreen as you look from the driver's seat*
- *listen and feel for any weird bump as you get near the curb and steer away if that is the case.*

12. Not looking around properly before moving off

This is something that is taught from the first lesson as it is a crucial part of safe driving. Checking all your surroundings including all the blind spots is essential before you move your car. Most people will check their mirrors a bit then forget to check their blind spots.

When moving off from the left, the right blind spot is very important as this is the direction you will be moving off into. If you fail to check and someone is there that you should have seen that will be a problem. Even if there is no one there, if you consistently fail to check your blind spots, you will get a serious fault for this.

How to avoid this fault:

- *Get your car ready to go before looking around (get into gear, have your biting point etc....)*
- *If you have looked and you can't move because it is busy, make sure you look again over your right shoulder just before you move off.*
- *If you were about to move off without checking and you suddenly remember, stop and check properly.*
- *If you have stalled whilst trying to move off, do your checks again as things could have changed by the time you are ready to move off again.*
- *Do not move off until you have checked over your blind spots.*

13. **Moving off into the path of another vehicle**

So you've done all your checks and everything looks good to go.

Are you sure?

Is there a car that looks far away but may be driving towards you really fast?

Are you on a narrow road and there are vehicles coming from the opposite direction?

If you move off, is there enough space for them so your actions don't affect them?

These are some of the questions you should be asking yourself before you make the decision to move off. Getting in the way of another vehicle can be:

- moving off and causing another road user to slow down.
- moving off in such a way that causes another driver to brake sharply or take evasive action to avoid an accident.

How to avoid this fault:

- *On narrow roads, look out for vehicles coming from the opposite direction, if they are close enough give them priority.*
- *Check for cyclists.*
- *If you are unsure about how fast a car is travelling towards you, just wait.*
- *Check your right mirror as you are moving off, cars might appear after you have made the decision to move. Checking your right mirror will allow you to see them before it is too late.*
- *Stop if you spot another vehicle which you might come into contact with.*

14. Driving off with the handbrake still applied

After doing your checks and it is safe for you to move off, releasing the handbrake can sometimes be overlooked. Not releasing the handbrake will not make you fail the test in itself unless you leave it on for too long. Leaving the handbrake on can have other consequences such as stopping your car as you move out into the road. This could put your car in the path of other vehicles and cause a hazardous obstacle.

How to avoid this fault:

- *Most cars have an alarm that tell you when the handbrake is still on, listen out for this.*
- *Look out for the red warning sign on the dashboard that tells you when the handbrake is on.*
- *Hold the handbrake as you look around so that you don't forget about it.*
- *If it feels a bit harder than normal to move the car then check your handbrake.*
- *If you realise you haven't released it, avoid slamming the brake, just keep the car moving if it is safe to do so and release the handbrake.*

15. Getting too close to parked car as you move off

Also known as an angled start, pulling over behind a parked car and then driving off again is part of the test. It is intended to test your control of the car as you move off. Getting too close to the car as you move off will get you a serious fault.

How to avoid this fault:

- *don't get too close when pulling over (One car length. A big car)*
- *don't move off too quickly*
- *don't come off the clutch until you have moved safely away from the car so that you can move off smoothly*

- *steer sharply*
- *if you have stopped too close by mistake, ask the examiner if you can reverse back a little bit.*

Car controls

Mastering the controls of a car is essential for driving safely. On the driving test, the examiner will want to see that you can control the car in a way that is safe. You don't need to be the smoothest with the controls, this comes with time. You do however need to demonstrate that you can control the car to a reasonable level.

Here are some faults to avoid:

16. Pressing the brake instead of the gas

This one is pretty self-explanatory. Pressing the brake when you are supposed to press the gas will make the car slow down too much. This will cause vehicles behind you to brake sharply or go into the back of your car. You don't want either of those.

17. Moving off in gear 3 or 2

Moving off in gear 2 is possible but you are more likely to stall. Moving off in gear 2 won't make you fail if you can manage it. Moving off in gear 3 on the other hand is another story altogether. This will not work. If it does it, will be very slow and loud.

Of course there are situations where you might want to move off in gear 2, such as down a really steep hill. I am not talking about that scenario. This fault applies when you are on a flat road or even a hill and forget to gear back down to 1 after stopping.

How to avoid this fault:

- *Get into the habit of going into gear 1 as you stop the car so that it becomes a part of your stopping routine.*
- *If you stall when moving off, check to make sure that it is not because you are in the wrong gear – the examiner will give you a chance but if you keep stalling and don't fix the gear issue, they may have to assist you.*
- *Don't bring your clutch up too quickly – this works if you are in gear 2 by mistake. It will allow you to move off in 2 provided that you are not on a steep hill and your car can manage it.*
- *Check each time after you stop that you are in gear 1.*

18. Not knowing how to turn on your windscreen wipers when it starts raining

If you are driving a car that is unfamiliar to you, it may be difficult to know how to operate certain things such as the windscreen wipers. You might start the driving test when it is dry and halfway through it starts to rain. If you don't clear the screen, your view of the road will be seriously affected. Could you think of a few consequences of having a windscreen you can't see out of?

How to avoid this fault:

- *Familiarise yourself with all the controls of the car.*
- *If in doubt and are already on the test, ask the examiner if you can pull over in a safe place and try to figure it out.*
- *Don't drive with the windscreen full of rain.*

19. Going into gear 1 when trying to go into gear 3

This usually happens when you are in gear 2, increasing your speed then going for gear 3. If you put the car into gear 1 by mistake at this stage the result can be a bit scary. When you lift the clutch up after the gear change, the car will slow down A LOT. If there is anybody following behind you, they may bump into you or get very close as they will not get any warning that your car is going to slow down drastically.

As you can imagine, this is a fault that if not dealt with properly will result in a serious fault being recorded.

How to avoid this fault:

- *When releasing the clutch after a gear change, do it slowly – this will allow you time to feel the gear you are in. If you are in the wrong gear and you lift the clutch all the way up, that gear will be engaged straight away and your speed will drop if it is gear 1. If you lift your clutch up slowly on the other hand, you will notice that the car is slowing down slightly and that will give you time to press down the clutch again and reapply the correct gear.*
- *Don't use too much force to get into gear 3 – when applying gear 3, the best way is to use little force. If you have to use a lot of force then the gearstick is probably stuck between 1 and 3, forcing it may push it into one.*
- *Change to gear 3 in two steps – instead of going to gear 3 in one big move from gear 2, try doing it in two moves. A gentle push up will put the gear stick into neutral. Make sure you let go of the gear stick before giving it another push up. Don't direct it left or right, just push straight up gently and you should get it in gear 3 smoothly.*

Mirrors

I think when it comes to driving, one of the things that almost all people will know is that it involves a lot of mirror checks. Knowing this and doing it are unfortunately two completely different things.

Here are a few mirror faults to avoid:

20. Not checking mirrors before signalling

Before you signal, it is important that you check your mirrors first. The correct order is:

Centre mirror then **Side mirror** of the direction you are going in, then **signal.**

If this is not done, you may miss things like cyclists beside you and signal which may startle them. Can you think what a cyclist might do if they are startled by you signal?

How to avoid this fault:

- *Practice this routine in your head: **Mirror**....**Mirror**....**Signal**.*
- *Check before you signal, not after.*
- *If you check your mirror and there is someone right by your side, don't signal straight away.*
- *When changing lanes, if there is a vehicle beside you in the lane you want to get into, let them go past you a bit before signalling. Signalling when they are right next to you might make them swerve.*

21. **Not checking your centre mirror before braking**

It is good practice to check your mirrors before changing direction. If you need to brake sharply for whatever reason, it is good to know how close the vehicle behind you is so that you can adjust your braking accordingly. (This does not apply to emergency braking where you are not expected to check your mirrors before stopping as there is not enough time in an emergency.) Not checking your mirror might make you brake in a way that causes a vehicle behind you to also brake sharply or worse, go into the back of your car.

How to avoid this fault:

- *plan ahead*
- *When you see any activity in the road that may require you to slow down or change direction, check your centre mirror*
- *even if you don't brake, check your centre mirror*
- *when approaching lights that have been green for a long time, check your centre mirror in case they change to red as you approach them.*

22. **Not checking the mirrors before changing direction**

Before you move left or right, it is necessary for you to check the mirror of the direction you are going to turn. There are a few ways in which this fault can occur:

- You fail to check the mirror altogether and miss another road user that is next to you.
- You check the mirror and see another vehicle but still drive into their path.
- You check the mirror but misjudge how far another vehicle is.

- You check the mirror but miss the vehicle beside you because it is in your blind spot.

How to avoid this fault:

- *check mirrors before changing direction*
- *If you have blind spot mirrors, use them to confirm that no one is in your blind spot.*
- *If you haven't got a blind spot, it may be worth doing a quick check over your shoulder to see if there is anybody in your blind spot.*
- *When changing direction because of an obstruction in your lane, be patient when trying to change lanes and only go if it is safe to do so.*
- *When you have pulled in for a meeting situation, use your right mirror before coming out again.*

Signals

Signals are what tell other people around you of your intentions. Not signalling correctly can have serious consequences for you and others. These are some of the most common ones to avoid:

23. Not signalling when necessary

Deciding whether to signal or not can be tricky sometimes. If you don't signal and someone could have benefited from that signal, you could cause confusion which can lead to an accident.

How to avoid this fault:

- *Ask yourself if there are any other people around that might benefit from your signal. If the answer is yes then you should signal.*
- *when changing lanes always signal*
- *when turning into or out of a road always signal.*

24. Signalling unnecessarily

Just like not signalling, signalling unnecessarily could be just as bad. An example that is quite common is people signalling to go around a stationary bus. This is not always a problem but imagine if there is a road on the right just past that bus. What will people think if they see your right signal on as you approach that road? If pedestrians see your right signal, they will think you are going to turn right. What do you think they might do?

How to avoid this fault:

- *ask yourself what your signal might be telling other people*
- *put yourself in other people's shoes and think about your signal*

- *people expect you to go around that bus anyway so do you really have to signal?*

25. **Signalling too early**

When approaching junctions, it is important that you signal at the correct time. Doing this correctly will avoid any confusion between you and other road users. On normal residential roads you should be signalling about 3 houses away from where you want to turn. You should signal earlier on faster roads. Before you signal, you need to make sure that there is no road in between where you are signalling and where you intend to turn. Going past a road on the left with a left signal on could be very dangerous.

Can you think what might happen if another driver was waiting on a side road, they see your left signal on but you don't turn into that road, what might that driver do when they see your signal?

How to avoid this fault:

- *Identify where you are going to turn before applying your signal.*
- *Make sure there are no roads in between where you are signalling and where you are turning.*
- *If you realise early enough that you have signalled too early, cancel it then reapply it when you get to the right place.*
- *Be clear about where you want to turn.*
- *If you are not sure ask the examiner.*

26. **Signalling too late**

Signalling too late can have serious consequences too. Imagine you are on a dual carriageway, a car in front of you intends to turn left but they only signal just as they are about to turn. You get no warning and now you have to slow down quite rapidly and maybe change direction. This can be dangerous. There are other scenarios where signalling late might cause issues. Can you think of any?

How to avoid this fault:

- *Make sure you know where you are turning in plenty of time.*
- *Signal earlier on faster roads.*
- *Get your mirrors and signal out of the way before worrying about gears as you approach a junction.*
- *If you remember a bit later than you should have, put the signal on as soon as you can.*

27. Not cancelling a signal after a turn

Some turns you do will require a lot of steering which will be enough to activate the signal cancelling mechanism. There are times when for whatever reason the signal doesn't cancel itself after you have completed a turn. It might be after exiting a roundabout for example. Having a signal on when it shouldn't be will definitely confuse other road users with the potential for an accident being high.

How to avoid this fault:

- *get used to cancelling your signal on your lessons*
- *listen to the clicking of the signal after you have turned*
- *if you can still hear a click, cancel it*
- *don't have your windows open too wide as this might prevent you from hearing the signal click.*

28. Not signalling correctly

This can come in many forms:

- not signalling to enter a roundabout when turning right
- not signalling to exit a roundabout
- not signalling to turn left or right at junctions
- signalling left when going right and vice versa.

Manoeuvres

On your driving test you will be asked to complete one reverse manoeuvre. This should demonstrate your ability to control your car in reverse in a safe manor. With enough practice, any of the four manoeuvres should be relatively easy.

There can be some issues and here are some to watch out for:

Bay parking

29. Finishing outside of the parking bay.

This applies to the reverse bay park as well as driving forward into a bay manoeuvre. When completing these manoeuvres, you must have all four wheels inside one bay that you have chosen to park in.

How to avoid this fault:

- *On the reverse bay park, use a reference point such as using the 3rd line from the bay you want to end up in as a turning point when it is in the middle of your driver's door.*
- *If you have ended up outside of the lines, you are allowed to make a correction. Bear in mind that you are only allowed to do this once so make it count.*
- *When making a correction, take your time to plan what you are going to do.*
- *When making a correction, use all the space you need, so reverse back far enough so you can see the lines and drive/reverse into the bay.*

30. Getting too close to another car on the bay park

As you do your test you will be asked to go into whichever bay you like. There may be other cars nearby and occasionally, the only option maybe to park next to another car. A serious fault will be recorded if you get so close to the vehicle that you are likely to hit it.

How to avoid this fault:

- *If there are lots of empty bays, choose one that is not close to another car.*
- *If you have to park next to another car, make sure you start wide. Starting really close to the bays will make it more likely that you will get close to the other car before going into your bay.*
- *If you can see that you are getting too close, stop before it is too late and make the necessary adjustments. Don't just leave it and hope for the best. You need to sort it out before the examiner has to intervene.*

31. Reversing/Driving forward too far into the bay

If you are not careful, this can be quite an easy mistake to make. You might be focussing on something else and forget that the back/front of the car is about to hit a barrier.

How to avoid this fault:

- *As you get near the end of the manoeuvre, cover your brakes so that you are ready to stop the car instantly.*
- *Keep an eye on the back of the car if reversing in, use blind spot mirrors if you have them to see where the back of your car is*
- *Use a reference point. When reversing, once in the bay, reverse back until the line in front of the car is underneath your wing mirror. This is usually a good time to stop.*

32. Not realising you are in the bay, making an unnecessary correction then ending up outside the bay

Yes this has happened before. A learner got the car into the bay perfectly, for some reason the learner thought her car wasn't in the bay and proceeded to make a correction. After she made the correction she finished with the car outside the bay and failed the test.

How to avoid this fault:

- *Only make a correction if your car is not inside the bay.*
- *Don't make a correction just to make the car straight or in the middle of the bay. As long as all four wheels are in the bay, leave it alone.*
- *Before making any correction, make sure that it is necessary.*

Parallel parking

33. Finishing too far from the pavement on a parallel park

This can happen if you are not sure how to get the car close enough to the pavement without mounting the pavement. A lot of learners are scared that they will hit the curb so they stay too far from it. Or simply misjudge how far they are from the curb.

How to avoid this fault:

- *don't be afraid to get close to the curb*
- *touching the curb slightly won't make you fail the test*
- *make corrections if necessary*
- *blind spot mirrors are a great way to see how far you are from the curb.*

34. Not finishing with your car straight

When parking, you need to finish in a position that does not obstruct other cars from driving past your car. It might seem like you are close enough to the pavement because the back wheel is really close to the curb, but where is the front of your car? If you are not careful, it might be sticking into the road. What might happen to your car if you leave it like this?

How to avoid this fault:

- *Look in your left mirror, if the gap between your car and the curb is not the same from the back of the car to the front, your car is probably wonky.*
- *Use the car that you are parking next to as a guide, your dashboard should be lined up with the car in front.*

35. Mounting the curb on a parallel park

So the point above said don't be afraid of the curb. This does not mean you can drive on to the curb. Where there is a dropped curb (the entrance to someone's driveway where the curb is lowered) this fault is much easier to make as you won't feel the car going over it. If you are not paying attention to where the back of the car is, you can easily end up on the pavement before you know it.

How to avoid this fault:

- *If you are parking next to a dropped curb, pay a lot of attention when you are closer to the curb to ensure that you do not reverse over it.*
- *If you feel a bit of resistance, i.e. the car is finding it a bit harder to keep reversing, you may have hit the curb. Don't force it, check to see where your back wheel is.*
- *If you are too close to the pavement, don't try to fix this by reversing. Drive forward and correct it.*

36. Getting too close to the car you are trying to park next to on the parallel park

When pulling up next to the car you are parking next to, it can be easy to lose focus of where your car is actually going as you try to get your reference point. This may result in you getting too close to the parked car. You might also get too close when reversing or making any correction.

How to avoid this fault:

- *When starting, make sure you are at least a door's width away from the parked car.*
- *On the reverse don't turn too early. Turning towards the curb when you have almost reversed past the parked car will make it a lot easier to keep away from the parked car.*
- *When making corrections, don't drive too close to the parked car, you would be better off going forward a bit and then reversing again.*
- *If you feel you are getting a bit close, stop the car and correct it before the examiner has to intervene.*

Right reverse

37. Reversing too far into the road when doing the reverse on the right

This is when you have been asked to pull over on the right hand side of the road. The examiner will say something like...

'When it is safe to do so, pull over on the right hand side of the road.'

After that you the will be told something like:

'I would like you to reverse back two car lengths keeping reasonably close to the curb.'

The key here is to keep the car close to the curb and not let it reverse out into the road.

How to avoid this fault:

- *When pulling in to the right side of the road, stop the car in such a way that you are not too far from the curb.*
- *Make sure the car is straight when stopping. If the back is sticking out towards the road then you will already be going towards the middle of the road as soon as you start reversing.*
- *Keep an eye on the mirror next to the curb (don't stare at it though).*
- *Use a reference in the rear window, to keep the car straight. This is usually when the curb is in the centre of the rear screen when you look at it through the rear view mirror. This may differ slightly depending on the car and how you sit.*

38. Not stopping for passing vehicles

This can apply to any of the reversing manoeuvres you may be asked to do. When doing a manoeuvre, you must stop for any vehicle or other road users that are close to your car. It may be that you have not looked around properly or just missed the road user you were supposed to see.

How to avoid this fault:

- *Before moving, check all around you.*
- *If you see any movement, keep an eye on it.*
- *Make an imaginary circle around your car so that if anybody gets inside it you will stop the car.*
- *Wait for the road user to leave the circle before continuing.*
- *Before continuing, make sure you do another all-round check, including all blind spots.*
- *Don't focus on one area such as the left mirror, keep your head moving and see what is around you the whole time.*

39. Just not looking around enough on manoeuvres

As mentioned above, looking around is very important. Even if there are no other road users around, you will still get a serious fault if you don't look around enough when doing a manoeuvre.

How to avoid this fault:

- *Don't be in a rush to complete the manoeuvre. Rushing usually means you might forget to look around.*
- *Don't look at one spot for too long.*
- *Look over your blind spots properly, not just your mirrors.*
- *If you find it hard to look around whilst reversing, just stop the car while you look around and then continue if it is safe. Repeat this until you have finished.*

Junctions

Junctions form a huge part of the driving test. If you lack the confidence to deal with all aspects of junctions then you should definitely get this sorted before going for your test. Because you will be dealing with a lot of junctions, there is a higher chance of making a mistake here during your test.

Here a quite a few of the most common ones to look out for:

40. Getting too close to parked car as you approach give way lines

On some sections of the test you may drive on narrow roads. If there are cars parked on the sides, you usually have to drive in the middle of the road. This can cause problems when you reach the end of the road and you are trying to position yourself on the correct side of the junction.

You have to be careful when driving past the last parked car. The problem is that you might turn too early, so early that your car gets very close to the last car. Of course it is important to position your car correctly but make sure that you have gone past the last car before turning to avoid turning into it.

How to avoid this fault:

- *approach the junction slowly*
- *check your left mirror before turning left*
- *check out of your left window to make sure that you have gone past the parked car*
- *if the last car is too close to the junction, you may have to position your car slightly over the centre line as you get to the give way lines (only do this if there is no other choice).*

41. Stopping too far past the give way lines

The give way lines are painted there to let you know that you must give way to other vehicles in the road you are about to join. Stopping too far past this line and going into the new road when approaching give way lines can cause a dangerous obstruction to the cars that have priority.

How to avoid this fault:

- *approach give way lines slowly*
- *Use a reference point. This is usually done by driving up to the end of the road and making sure the give way lines look like they are under your wing mirror when you look out of the driver's window.*
- *If you can't see into the new road without going over the give way lines, don't just go over it straight away. Use the peep and creep technique (Peep your head forward as far you can, if you can't see creep your car a little bit forward.) Repeat this process until you can see into the road.*

42. Pulling out in front of a vehicle that has priority

When dealing with junctions, there will often be situations where you have to give priority to other road users. Driving out in front of another vehicle that has priority can be very dangerous, especially if the other driver is not expecting it. Can you think what might happen if you pull out in front of a car that has priority?

This can happen for several reasons:

- you might misjudge how far an approaching vehicle is
- you might not look properly
- you might look but miss something like a cyclist
- A car might be turning into your road but you fail to consider the car behind them which will come rushing towards you once the turning car has started turning.

How to prevent this fault:

- *When judging whether to emerge or not, use the walk across drive across rule. (Imagine you are a pedestrian where your car is, if you check the road and you would cross the road then you can drive across)*
- *Before emerging, look both left and right a few times before making a decision.*
- *Look out for cyclists as they are harder to see. Make sure you allow for anything that may be hidden by your windscreen pillars.*
- *When a car is turning into the road you are emerging from, make sure you take into account any vehicles that might be behind them which might come towards you.*
- *If there are parked cars blocking your view, give it a few seconds for any vehicles that may be hidden by the parked cars.*

43. Approaching a junction too fast

When approaching a junction, you want to drive at a speed that will allow you to do everything correctly such as checking your mirrors, signalling and turning safely. If you approach too fast, you will increase the likelihood of causing an accident.

How to prevent this fault:

- *make sure you know where the junction is*
- *if you are in a high gear, gear down before you get to your turn*
- *brake early to reduce your speed gradually*

44. Approaching a junction using two lanes unnecessarily

Some junctions have more than one lane to allow traffic to flow more smoothly. When approaching a junction, the lane you are in may split into more than one lane. Learners sometimes have their vehicle in two lanes, blocking other traffic from using that lane.

How to prevent this fault:

- *As you approach, make sure you check if it is one or two lanes.*
- *Decide which lane you are going to use nice and early.*
- *You would be better off in the wrong lane and going that way than straddling two lanes.*

45. Using the wrong lane to turn left or right

It is important to look at the road markings as you might be in a lane that is for turning left only but you want to go straight.

What could be the consequences of using the wrong lane?

Where will other drivers expect you to go if you are in a left only lane?

How to avoid this fault:

- *Read road markings as you approach the junction.*
- *Approach the junction at a speed that allows you to see the lanes and plan properly.*
- *If you find yourself in the wrong lane, it might be safer just to go in the direction where that lane takes you (as long as it is not leading to a motorway).*
- *If it safe to do so, you can check your mirrors, signal and change to the correct lane.*

46. Positioning too far left/right on a junction

When turning from a minor road onto a major road, it is important that you position the car correctly. This will allow other cars to use the junction to go the other way. If you are positioned badly, other drivers won't able to go around you and may become annoyed.

How to prevent this fault:

- *If turning left, make sure you position your car towards the left side of the junction.*
- *If turning right, position yourself as far right as possible without going over the centre line.*
- *If the junction is very small, don't worry if other cars can't use the space beside you. They will just have to wait until you have moved.*

47. Taking too long to emerge

This doesn't happen as often as you might think. Often learners want to rush out because they feel like they are taking too long. It is better to take your time but if you take too long then it might be a problem. I'm talking about waiting for vehicles that are so far away that you will not affect them if you come out.

How to avoid this fault:

Use the walk across drive across rule. (Explained above)

48. Stopping unnecessarily when you have priority

On crossroads it can be easy to mistake who has priority if you unfamiliar with the rules. Sometimes you might know that you have priority but a car may come towards the junction a bit faster than you expect, causing you to stop for them suddenly. This can cause other cars behind you to stop suddenly or go into the back of your car as they will not expect you to stop.

How to avoid this fault:

- *When approaching crossroads, check to see if the give way lines are in front of your car (if they are then you must give way).*
- *If a car is coming from the side at speed and you have priority, cover your brake (have your foot over the brake pedal) but don't stop unless they get in your way.*

- *Before deciding to stop, always check your centre mirror for any cars that may be following closely behind.*

49. Turning too slowly in front of an oncoming vehicle

You are waiting to turn right into a minor road from a major road. You see a nice gap in the traffic so you take your chance and start moving to make the turn. If you go so slowly that the oncoming vehicle now has to slow down for you, this will be a serious fault. Can you think of any consequences that may occur as a result of moving too slowly when making a turn? What might slowing the other drivers do?

How to avoid this fault:

- *Make sure there is a nice enough gap before attempting to turn. Use walk across drive across rule.*
- *If in a manual car, have your car ready to go: Use the handbrake, get a decent amount of gas on and get your clutch to the biting point. This will allow you to move off smoothly.*

50. Cutting corners

Cutting corners is one of those faults that you may not even realise you have done if you are not paying attention. This is when you are turning right from a main road into a side road and you turn too early. This will cause your car to go into the lane for cars coming out of the road you are turning into. Think of what might happen if you turn into a lane that is meant for oncoming vehicles.

How to avoid this fault:

- *Before turning, make sure the centre line of the road you are trying to turn into is in line with the right wing mirror. This will mean that you are in a good position to turn.*

- *If there are vehicles parked in the junction which prevent you from turning on your side of the road, you may cut the corner, only do this if it is clear and do so slowly.*

51. Turning too wide unnecessarily

Turning too wide might mean that you go into the wrong side of the road and possibly cause other vehicles to brake or swerve. It might also mean that you get too close to the curb or can't make the turn.

How to avoid this fault:

- *Control your speed before turning as this is a big cause of turning wide.*
- *Steer quickly if the turn is sharp.*
- *If you notice you are going to be wide, just slow down smoothly and turn more.*

52. Braking too sharply just before turning

You are about to turn, there's a car behind you and that driver has seen you are going to turn, they expect you to turn so they can carry on driving straight. If you suddenly brake sharply, the driver behind won't anticipate that and might hit the back of your car.

How to avoid this fault:

- *start braking early*
- *don't wait until you get to the turn to start using your brakes*
- *If there is a car following closely behind you, slow down gradually so that they will be going slow as well.*
- *If you don't know exactly where the turn is, slow down a bit and ask the examiner as they may be able to show you. This will help you to know where it is and plan earlier.*
- *If you realise too late where the turn is and you are going too fast. It may be safer to continue without turning (Provided no one gets*

confused by your signal and emerges in front of you because they think you are going to turn).

53. Stopping unnecessarily for pedestrians that are on the pavement as you turn.

This is linked to the point above but it is a bit more specific.

How to avoid this fault:

- *Check your mirrors for any vehicles that may be following close behind you.*
- *If the pedestrian is still on the pavement then don't stop.*
- *Make eye contact with pedestrians.*
- *If they are jogging or not paying attention then slow down a bit more to see what they do.*

54. Turning into a no entry road

As crazy as that sounds it does happen. As you do your driving test, there may be turns where you are asked to go which are right next to a no entry road. The mistake learners make is failing to see the no entry sign and trying to turn down that road.

How to avoid this fault:

- *Be clear about where you intend to turn – if in doubt, ask the examiner beforehand and they will make it clearer where the turn is.*
- *Look out for give way lines – you shouldn't turn into a road that has double give way lines the whole way across the entrance of that road. This is a big clue that you shouldn't be turning into that road.*
- *Look out for the no entry sign – sounds obvious but this is the best way to avoid this fault. The signs are red for a reason.*

Traffic lights

55. Stopping dangerously for orange lights.

Deciding if you should stop when the light is orange can be very tricky. The mistake occurs if you see an orange light when you are very close to the lights, panic and slam the brakes on. If a vehicle is behind you, this could be potentially dangerous as the driver behind you may not expect you to stop so suddenly and may have been planning to go through that orange light after you.

How to prevent this fault:

- *Check your mirror before making a decision.*
- *Practice and have a point of no return. This is a point where you don't stop if the light goes orange.*
- *Don't speed up to make it through a green light. Doing this will increase the likelihood of you having to brake harshly should the lights change.*
- *If you see that the lights have been green for a long time as you approach them, be ready for them to change and start slowing down slightly.*

IMPORTANT NOTE: If the light is red you must stop. Do not go through a red light. With careful planning and awareness you should be able avoid this situation.

56. Not stopping for a red light.

As obvious as this sounds it does happen. When people are under stress they can miss red lights. This happens a lot at roundabouts that are controlled by lights. If the lights are in the middle of the roundabout it can be easy to miss when you are focused on going round the roundabout and thinking about your exit.

Temporary traffic lights are often ignored by learner drivers for reasons that no one has ever been able to explain to me. I have asked a few learners who have almost gone through the temporary red light during our lessons. The answer that I get is something along the lines of… "I did see it but I don't know, I didn't think it applied to me."

How to prevent this fault:

- *Look out for temporary lights that apply to you.*
- *Make sure you look for the sign that tells you where to stop.*
- *When approaching a red light, keep an eye on the stop line and take care not to go past the line.*

57. Not going when the light is green

This sounds silly I know. It can happen when the driver is waiting at a red light, the light changes to green and they don't move because they are not paying attention and don't realise it's green.

Another way this can happen, which I see quite a lot is when there is a filter light. This is where there is an arrow that turns green to allow one set of drivers go left, right or straight while the others have to wait. The driver may only see the red light which doesn't apply to them and miss the green one for them.

How to prevent this fault:

- *If you are first at the lights, don't lose focus and start looking around too much.*
- *Keep an eye on the lights so that when they change you will see them.*

- *When approaching a junction with a lot of lights, keep an eye out for filter lights and make sure you are not stopping for the wrong light.*

58. Getting stuck in the middle of the junction when turning right at lights

When turning right at traffic lights, having cars in front of you that are also turning right before you can make it trickier. You need to decide whether there is enough space for you to go forward and wait or if you should wait behind the stop line. If you go forward but there is not enough space, you run the risk of being stuck in the middle when the light goes red for you and green for the traffic coming from the sides. If this happens you may cause an obstruction which can be dangerous and cost you your test.

How to avoid this fault:

- *If you are behind cars that also want to turn right, make sure there is enough space for you in the middle of the junction.*
- *Don't go past the stop line if there isn't enough space for you.*
- *Don't block the pedestrian crossing section.*
- *If there is no space after the pedestrian crossing section, wait behind the stop line*
- *Don't have your car half way over the stop line.*
- *Either wait behind the stop line or after the pedestrian crossing section if there is one.*
- *Keep an eye on the lights so you can go when it's safe.*

59. Following other vehicles when the light is red

When waiting at lights in traffic, sometimes the light might be green but you can't go because there is heavy traffic. You must keep an eye on the lights before going through as they may have changed to red without you realising, especially if other cars have gone forward.

How to avoid this fault:

- *Don't go past the stop line without looking at the lights first.*
- *Don't blindly follow the car in front of you.*
- *If the light is amber going to red then wait until the next green light.*

<u>Speed</u>

60. **Going too slowly**

Sometimes, learners on test think that if they drive slowly throughout, they can't make any mistakes and won't fail because they are driving safely. This is not true. You should always drive at the appropriate speed for the conditions.

Some learners are not comfortable with driving at high speeds. This can be a real issue if your test takes you onto the dual carriageway. On some dual carriageways the speed limit can be 70mph so it is best that you practice driving at those speeds before going for your test. You wouldn't want to pass your test and not be able to drive at high speeds.

It is important that you lookout for speed limit changes. It's very easy to drive too slowly because you are not sure of the speed limit.

How to avoid this fault:

- *Make sure you know what the speed limit is for the road you are driving on.*
- *If you realise that you are driving too slow, you can increase your speed gradually.*

61. **Not overtaking slow moving vehicles**

This usually happens on dual carriageways. If a bus or slow moving lorry is in front of you and the other lanes are clear, you should overtake it.

How to avoid this fault:

- *plan ahead*

- *If you see a vehicle in the distance moving slowly, start checking your mirrors early and if you get close because the vehicle is still moving slowly, start to go around if it is safe to do so.*
- *If the other lanes are really busy then it may not be appropriate to overtake.*
- *If you are planning to turn left soon then overtaking may not be appropriate.*

62. Driving too fast

You don't necessarily have to be driving over the speed limit to be driving too fast. Often it can be when the road is a bit narrow or there is a lot going on but you fail to reduce your speed to match the conditions of that road.

The speed limit is important and if you go over it by too much then you will get a serious fault. You can also get a serious fault if you consistently go over the speed limit even by a couple of MPH.

How to avoid this fault:

- *Look out for when the road narrows.*
- *Take a glance at your speedometer to make sure you are not going over the speed limit by mistake.*
- *If a Sat Nav is set up in the car, this will tell you the speed limit on most roads so use it.*
- *If you are not sure about the speed, don't go fast straight away.*
- *If you go over slightly the examiner may remind you what the speed limit is and you will get a minor fault.*
- *If you go over too quickly, say 30MPH in a 20MPH ZONE, you will get a serious fault.*

Positioning

When driving, it is important that you are aware of the car's position at all times. You might be aware of where your car is but unaware that you shouldn't be there. Here are some positional faults to avoid:

63. Getting too close to parked cars

Unfortunately this happens a lot. It is one of those faults that you won't realise you have made until the test is finished. Unless you get so close that the examiner has to steer the car for you to avoid hitting a parked car.

You should be driving in a position that will allow someone in a parked car to open their door without you hitting them as you drive past.

This fault often happens when learners have pulled in to the left to let an oncoming vehicle past in a meeting situation and as they move back out they fail to steer enough and get too close the parked car.

How to avoid this fault:

- *When driving through very narrow gaps, go slower.*
- *Check the left as you go past parked cars.*
- *When pulling in for a meeting situation, make sure you give yourself plenty of room to move off again so that you don't get too close when moving off again.*
- *If you have to get close to a parked car for any reason, make sure you are going very slowly.*
- *Go through some width restrictions on your lessons so that you know exactly how wide your car is and you can manoeuver in tight gaps.*

64. Driving too close to the vehicle in front

Another fault that is easy to miss. In normal conditions you should drive at least 2 seconds from the vehicle in front. Double that when it is wet and 10 times if it is icy. (you are unlikely to go on a driving test if the roads are icy)

During the driving test, you will be focusing on so many things that you might fail to realise that you are following too closely to the vehicle in front of you.

How to avoid this fault:

- *Use a fixed marker like a lamppost, when the vehicle in front of you goes past that post you start counting. If you reach that post before you get to 2 seconds then you are too close. Back off.*
- *If a car comes in the gap that you have between you and another vehicle in front of you, drop your speed slightly so that you can create a new safe gap.*
- *If you realise you are driving a little too close, you can save it before it's too late. Start reducing your speed and you may prevent a serious fault being recorded.*

Lanes

Whether it is a dual carriageway or not, there are some roads that have more than one lane going in the same direction. Knowing which lane to be in (or not to be in.) is a skill you must practice and become comfortable with before going for your driving test. Here are some of the faults associated with lanes:

65. Driving in the middle or right lane unnecessarily

This is another one of those faults you might not even realise you are committing.

The lane for normal driving is the left one. If you drive in the middle or right lane unnecessarily for too long you will get a serious fault. Although a lot people call the right lane the fast lane, it is actually an overtaking lane. It still has the same speed limit as the other lanes. For that reason, if you are in that lane unnecessarily, you could be blocking people that want to overtake and forcing them to undertake.

There may be times when the examiner will ask you to move to the middle or right lane or follow a particular direction which will require you to change lanes. This is fine and you should do it when it is safe to do so. Often the left lane will be going somewhere else and you might for example go over a flyover. After that flyover or bridge the road you are on might turn into 3 lanes again. If this is the case and you find yourself in the middle or right lane, you should make your way back to the left lane as soon as it is safe to do so. To give you a hint the examiner might say something like… "back to normal driving." Which basically means go back to the left lane when it safe to do so.

There are times that you should be using the right lane:

- when overtaking
- if there is an obstruction in the left lane
- when you are going to turn right
- when instructed to do so by examiner
- when following signs for a particular direction.

How to avoid this fault:

- *When turning onto a dual carriageway, always aim for the left lane.*
- *If you find you are in the middle or right lane and you shouldn't be there, make efforts to go back to the left as soon as it is safe.*
- *If you see people undertaking you (overtaking from the left) this should be a sign that you may be in the wrong lane.*

66. Driving in a bus lane when it is in operation

When dealing with bus lanes, it is crucial that you know what you are doing. Driving a bus lane when it is in operation will result in a serious fault unless there is a good reason to drive in there.

How to avoid this fault.

- *Get used to reading bus lane signs that tell you the times the bus lane is in operation.*
- *If you miss the sign that tells you the times, don't drive in it.*
- *Look out for signs that say "use the bus lanes", this means you can ignore the operational times of the bus lane.*
- *If turning left and you have to go past a bus lane to make the turn, wait for the thick white line of the bus lane to end or break before turning.*
- *Don't go into the bus lane just to make a left turn.*

67. Not using a bus lane when it is not in operation

This will not usually get you a serious fault on its own. If you don't use the bus lane when you should and other drivers start undertaking you from the bus lane, you may get a serious fault.

How to avoid this fault:

- *Check the bus lane times on the blue board.*
- *If the bus lane is clear, use it.*
- *If you realise late that you should be in the bus lane, it might not be too late, check your mirrors, signal and go into the bus lane when it is clear.*

68. Not checking your mirrors when lanes are merging together

Often two lanes will merge into one lane. It can be easy to not realise that this is happening. If you are unaware that lanes are merging, you might not see a car on your side that is going into the same space as you.

How to avoid this fault:

- *Look out for signs that lanes are merging.*
- *Lanes usually merge after traffic lights.*
- *Look ahead, if cars are going into a single file it is likely that the lanes are merging.*
- *If you are in the left lane check the right mirror and vice versa.*
- *Look on the floor for arrows that tell you the lanes are merging.*

69. Undertaking

Undertaking is one of those topics that many people don't know much about. Simply put, undertaking is overtaking from the left and it's not allowed. There are exceptions to this. You can undertake if:

- driving on a one way road
- the other traffic in the right is going slowly because of traffic and you can go past them slowly.

How to avoid this fault:

- *Be conscious of the fact that you might be undertaking as often people don't even realise that they are doing it.*
- *If someone is in the right lane going slowly, don't be tempted to go past them just because you want to drive at the speed limit.*
- *If someone is driving really slowly in the middle lane, you may have to make your way to the right lane to overtake them properly then go back to the left. Only do this if you are not going to be turning left soon.*
- *Let the examiner know of your intentions.*

70. Taking too long to go into a slip road when coming off a dual carriageway

Slip roads are designed to keep traffic moving by allowing you to maintain your speed whilst getting off the main road. This allows other cars behind you that are going straight to go without slowing down too much for you while you come off. If you don't use the slip road to do this, or have your vehicle hanging over the slip road and the left lane unnecessarily, you will prevent the other cars from going past you

How to avoid this fault:

- *Go into the slip road as early as possible.*
- *Don't wait until the slip road is big enough to fit your whole car, go in it from the start without getting too close to the edge of the road.*
- *Use your mirrors to check that your car is fully out of the left lane.*
- *Use a reference point to keep close to the edge of the road.*

Roundabouts

I can't imagine a driving test where a roundabout isn't involved. Learners often fear roundabouts and treat them like they are this big scary thing. In reality, roundabouts are quite straight forward once you practice them a bit. Look out for these common faults:

71. **Not realising there is a roundabout**

In order to deal with a roundabout properly, you have to first realise there is a roundabout. Some mini roundabouts are very difficult to see. If you go through a roundabout without looking to your right or realising that there is a roundabout, you will fail as this can be very dangerous. If you don't pay attention you may miss even larger roundabouts or realise too late that you have already entered the roundabout.

How to avoid this fault:

- *Look out for warning signs that tell you when approaching a roundabout.*
- *Look out for where other drivers in front you are slowing down, this may be a roundabout.*
- *Most mini roundabouts have a blue circle sign next to them, so look out for these.*

72. **Stopping too far into the roundabout**

This is linked to the fault above. If you see the roundabout late, it may cause you to stop too late. You might see the roundabout in good time but misjudge where to stop. Can you think of the consequences of stopping too far into a roundabout? Think about what it might cause other drivers to do.

How to avoid this fault:

- *Make sure you know where the give way line is.*
- *Don't creep into the roundabout until you are sure it is safe to go (unless you can't see the right and you have to use the peep and creep technique).*
- *Bring the give way line under your wing mirror as a reference point.*

73. Hesitating to go when you have priority

A test can make you second guess yourself at times. You might know full well that you have to give way to vehicles coming from the right but forget at the crucial point. Waiting for vehicles on the left when the right is clear is one of the most common ways to make this fault.

You may also make this fault if the vehicles on the right are being blocked by other vehicles that have priority over them but you still keep waiting.

How to avoid this fault:

- *Don't give way to people on the left of the roundabout when the right is clear.*
- *If vehicles on your right are blocked by other traffic, look for a chance to go.*
- *Look out for people's signals, if more than one car is turning left you should have time to go.*

74. Rushing into a roundabout

When dealing with roundabouts, it is important that you take the appropriate time to judge when it is safe to go. Rushing and going at the wrong time may cause dangerous situations.

How to avoid this fault:

- *Only go when you are 100% sure it is safe to do so.*
- *Don't be pressured into going by anybody behind you.*

- *Don't pay too much attention to the person behind you as this may add unnecessary pressure and cause you to go when it is unsafe.*
- *If somebody beeps at you, don't go unless it is safe.*

75. Stalling in the middle of a roundabout

This can happen for several reasons. Either because you have moved off using the wrong gear or just poor coordination of the pedals when moving off. Stalling in itself will not make you fail but stalling when you are in the path of other vehicles can lead to a serious fault.

How to avoid this fault:

- *come off the clutch smoothly*
- *make sure you are in the correct gear before moving off*
- *If you stall, restart your car as soon as you can and move off if it is safe to do so before getting in the way of other vehicles.*

76. Treating a double roundabout as a single roundabout

When dealing with double roundabouts. It is important to treat each one individually. It can be easy to forget that there is another roundabout after dealing with the first one. As you can imagine this can be quite dangerous.

How to avoid this fault:

- *Look out for signs that show the diagram of the roundabouts.*
- *If you are going in a direction that will take you through the second roundabout, don't forget to check the right again as you approach the second roundabout.*
- *Don't go too fast after the first roundabout.*

77. Driving over a roundabout

This is usually at mini roundabouts. You might fail to see that there is a roundabout and go over it without going around or you might see other cars going over it and just follow them.

How to avoid this fault:

- *Look out for roundabout signs.*
- *Don't drive over the white circle unless there is good reason to.*
- *Position your car well before going to the roundabout so that you don't steer straight into the circle.*

Pedestrians

On most test routes that you get, you will interact with pedestrians in some way or another. Depending on where you are and what time it is, the amount of interaction may differ. Knowing how to deal with pedestrians properly will not only make you more relaxed, it will make you a safer driver. Here are some faults to do with pedestrians you should avoid:

78. Not stopping for a pedestrian on a zebra crossing

Pedestrians crossing or waiting at a zebra crossing should be given priority. If you don't stop for someone that is either on the crossing or waiting to cross, the examiner will have to intervene.

How to avoid this fault:

- *Look out for zebra crossings from early on.*
- *Watch out for flashing orange beacons that warn you of a pedestrian crossing.*
- *Some have signs a few hundred yards before them.*
- *If your view of any of the sides of the crossing is obstructed, slow down a lot, only proceed once you are sure that there is no one waiting to cross.*
- *Slow down when approaching a crossing and if there are people around it or heading towards the crossing.*
- *If somebody is standing near the crossing, always assume that they want to cross, stop for them and if they still don't cross then proceed with care, making eye contact with them if possible.*

79. Stopping for pedestrians that are on the pavement where there is no pedestrian crossing

Where possible, pedestrians should cross using official pedestrian crossings such as zebra, pelican or puffin. Having a pedestrian that looks like they are about to cross can be scary. It can make you feel like they are going to cross the road. In a panic, it can be quite easy to stop for them when you don't really need or have to. If you stop for a pedestrian when you are not supposed to, other drivers behind you are unlikely to expect that you will stop.

How to avoid this fault:

- *Only stop if pedestrians actually step in the road.*
- *If they look like they are not paying attention, be prepared to stop and try to make eye contact with them.*
- *If they stay on the pavement keep driving.*
- *Learn to trust that pedestrians will do the right thing.*

80. Not stopping for pedestrians that are already on the road

This fault usually happens when approaching the end of the road before turning. Pedestrians may walk into the road because they know you are going to slow down to check the new road before turning. When you are so focused on watching out for any cars in the new road, it can be very easy to miss pedestrians that are right in front of your car. They may also be hidden by the windscreen pillar.

How to avoid this fault:

- *Before approaching the end of the road, check for any pedestrians that may already be crossing.*
- *Check for any pedestrians that may be hidden behind the windscreen pillar by moving your head.*
- *If there are any pedestrians crossing the road, they have priority, give them room to cross and proceed to the give way line when it is clear.*

- *Once it is clear, move forward to the give way line, this will allow any other pedestrians to cross behind your car rather than in front of the car.*

81. Blocking a pedestrian crossing

When in traffic, you must keep pedestrian crossings clear. If you are not careful, you may end up blocking a pedestrian crossing. Blocking pedestrian crossings isn't just annoying for pedestrians, it can have some other more serious consequences.

What if people can't cross where they are supposed to cross because you are blocking the way, where will they cross? What about wheel chair users or parents with buggies?

How to avoid this fault:

- *Look out for pedestrian crossings.*
- *Don't follow the vehicle in front too closely, you should leave enough space so that you can clearly see what is written on the floor.*
- *Don't drive forward unless you know you have enough space to clear the crossing.*
- *When turning right at lights, don't wait on the section where pedestrians cross, wait either behind the line or after the pedestrian crossing.*

There are times where you have to stop on a pedestrian crossing. This is usually on junctions that have a pedestrian crossing right by the give way line.

Other road users

82. Waiting behind a dustbin truck unnecessarily (A dustbin truck that is stationary because it is collecting rubbish)

This one is not so straight forward and can be quite tricky. If you can see that there is space and it is safe to continue you should go.

83. Rushing to go around a dustbin truck

Sounds contradictory especially after I said you can fail for waiting behind a dustbin truck but this is also another fault that can cause a test fail. The scenario is usually a busy morning, there is a dustbin truck in the way, you can't really see around it properly but you go around it anyway because you are anxious or are worried about holding the people behind you up. As you make your move to go, a car comes from the opposite direction and now you are in their way on their side of the road. Awkward to say the least.

How to avoid this fault:

- *If you can't see that it is clear around the dustbin truck then don't go.*
- *Position your car in a way that allows you to see around the dustbin truck without blocking oncoming traffic.*

84. Overreacting to a vehicle that is reversing on the other side of the road

A car reversing out of a driveway on the other side of the road should not affect you but because of test nerves, you might decide to suddenly stop for it. This will cause problems for vehicles following you.

- *If you see a vehicle reversing out of a driveway, reduce your speed slightly.*
- *Only stop if you can see that they are going to go into your lane.*
- *Try to make eye contact with the other driver if possible.*

85. Overtaking a cyclist just before turning left

When turning left, it can be made more challenging if there is a cyclist in front of you. You might feel like if you wait behind the cyclist then you will be going too slowly. If you are going to turn left however, it is not a good idea to overtake a cyclist just before you turn. Can you think what might happen if you turn just as you go past a cyclist?

How to avoid this fault:

- *If there is a cyclist in front of you and you know you are going to turn left, do not overtake them.*
- *If the turn is far enough away and the cyclist is going slowly then it might be ok to overtake then turn.*
- *If you are not sure, don't overtake.*
- *Signal and keep your distance from them.*

86. Waiting behind a bus unnecessarily

Buses often pull over to pick up and drop off passengers. If you stop and wait behind each time a bus did this you would never get anywhere in time. If there is space to go around a bus whilst it is at a bus stop you should go for it. If you don't go around a bus when you should, can you think what other drivers behind you might think? What might the other drivers try to do?

How to avoid this fault:

- *Don't follow the bus too closely.*
- *Watch out for the bus's signal, when it signals left to stop at a bus stop, reduce your speed slightly, keep as right as you can without going across the centre line, check for oncoming traffic and if clear check your right mirror before going around the bus. You do not need to signal for this.*

87. Not giving way to a bus that is pulling out of a bus stop

When buses are moving off from a bus stop, they have priority. If you see their signal and you have time to slow down or stop safely, you should let them out. Failing to do this could result in a serious fault.

How to avoid this fault:

- *When approaching a bus that is at a bus stop, keep an eye on its signals.*
- *Check your centre mirror for vehicles that may be following behind you.*
- *If the bus signals right and there is time to slow down safely to let it out then do so.*
- *If the bus signals right as you are about to go around it then it is usually safe to keep going.*

Meeting traffic

There are a lot of narrow roads in urban settings. Some of these are so narrow that there is not enough space for two vehicles to pass each other. This is where you get meeting situations. One driver will have to stop to let the other pass.

Here are some rules to help you get this right:

- The side with the obstruction usually gives way
- If there are obstructions on both sides, no one has priority
- If you have space on your side, you pull over on your side and let the other driver pass
- If the space is on the other side, you can stop and let the other driver go into that space
- Pull over into spaces on the left

88. Not stopping in a meeting situation when you don't have priority

On a narrow road, if you notice a parked vehicle obstructing your lane you will want to go around it. If there are cars coming from the opposite direction and their lane is clear, you should be very careful not to get in their way. If you get in their way and force them to stop, slow down or swerve you may get a serious fault. If the road is wide enough for you and the other driver to pass each other whilst you go past the obstruction then this is fine.

How to avoid this fault:

- *Check for oncoming vehicles before going around an obstacle.*
- *If you are unsure about the space, wait.*
- *If the other car has stopped to let you go past then you may go.*
- *Don't rush to go around obstacles if the road is busy.*

89. Not stopping when even though you have priority

Sounds weird I know. Just because you have priority doesn't mean that other drivers will give you priority. Imagine this scene:

You are driving along, there are no obstructions on your side of the road. You notice there is an obstruction on the opposite side of the road. There is another car approaching it from the opposite direction. You know that they should stop and let you carry on in your lane. They are not slowing down and they go into your lane to go past their obstruction. You don't do anything about it because you couldn't react quickly enough. The examiner has to press the brakes. You get a serious fault. Whose fault was it? You are angry because you had priority. Seems a bit unfair but that's how driving is sometimes. You have to be ready to deal with people that might not know or want to follow the rules.

How to avoid this fault:

- *Look at the speed of the other car.*
- *If they are not slowing down they may be planning to go around the obstacle using your lane.*
- *Cover your brake.*
- *Check your centre mirror to see if there is anyone following close behind you.*
- *If they go into your lane and there is not enough space for both of you, you will have to take control of the situation and stop your car.*

90. Not sharing the road

This is linked to the fault above. Imagine the same scene but this time you have more space of your side. Even though technically you have priority, because you have so much space, the other driver will see this and expect you to move over a little bit so that they can use a bit of your lane to go around the obstruction on their side. If you don't move over, the other driver might get very close to you or worse, clip your car.

How to avoid this fault:

- *Check the size of your lane as you approach obstructions.*
- *If there is another vehicle coming from the opposite direction, start to move to the left slightly as they will start to move into your lane.*
- *Check your left mirror before moving left.*

Awareness and planning

A lot of driving is basically being aware of what is going on around you and planning for things that might happen as you drive along. This takes practice. The more you drive the more you will be aware of your surroundings as you drive. Look out for these faults:

91. Mistaking parked cars for a line of traffic and stopping behind them

The difference between parked cars and a line of traffic can be very difficult to notice. If you are not careful, you might find yourself waiting behind parked cars and wondering why no one is moving. This shows lack of awareness.

How to avoid this fault:

- *Look for brake lights: In traffic, people tend to have their feet on the brakes as they are waiting. If the row of cars you are approaching has no brake lights at all, it is likely they are all parked and no one is in them.*
- *Just because one car has brake lights on doesn't mean that they are in traffic.*
- *Look for folded mirrors: Drivers often fold their mirrors in when they park their cars to avoid losing their mirror to another vehicle that is driving too closely. Use this as a sign that the cars you are approaching are in fact parked.*

92. Mistaking a row of traffic for parked cars and driving past them

This is tied in to the point above. If you are not paying attention, you might not realise there is traffic ahead of you. If you mistake cars that are in traffic for parked cars and drive past them, you might be going into oncoming traffic. By the time you realise, you may already have a vehicle heading straight for you.

You will be lucky if you spot each other and stop in time. Now the awkward bit, you have to reverse back all the way to the start of the queue of traffic you just went past. Fortunately, most examiners won't let it go that far. You will be stopped before you go past the queue of traffic resulting in a serious fault.

How to avoid this fault:

- *If in doubt, reduce speed slightly so that you have more time to read the situation.*
- *Check what the other vehicles in front of you are doing: Are they going around this row of cars or not?*
- *If you have to go to the other side of the road then check properly to see if the cars you are going past are parked or not.*
- *Look out for a lot of brake lights: if the line of cars has a lot of brake lights it is likely they are in a traffic queue.*
- *Look for indicators.*
- *Look for smoke coming from the exhausts of the vehicles in the queue.*

Show me Tell me

Before the test changes in 2017, you couldn't really fail on the show me tell me section of the test. Getting the answer wrong would have got you a minor fault. Now since some of the show me questions are asked whilst you are driving, you can make mistakes that will lead to a serious fault if you are not careful. Here are some of them:

93. Losing control of your steering

As you try to figure out which button does what, it can be very easy to lose focus and lose control of your steering. This can be serious as you may be driving into danger without even realising it.

How to avoid this fault:

- *Get to know what all the controls do before you go for your test.*
- *Practice the show me questions as you drive.*
- *If you don't know where a button is, ask the examiner if you can pull over in a safe place so that you can try and figure it out.*
- *Safety is number one. If you are really unsure then just leave it and focus on controlling the car.*

94. Losing control of your speed

Focussing on demisting the front window might require a lot of your concentration, especially if you are unfamiliar with the car. This might cause you to lose focus of your speed and either go too fast or too slow, creating issues for other drivers and a danger to other road users.

How to avoid this:

- *As you demonstrate and answer the question, keep an eye on your speed.*

- *If you feel your speed dropping, gradually bring it back up again.*
- *Listen to the tone of your engine, if you hear it changing as you do this exercise it is very likely that your speed is dropping or increasing.*
- *Do this exercise in a safe place. Don't do it where there are loads of things happening.*

Independent driving

The independent driving section of the driving test is often dreaded by learners who have never done it. It sounds a lot scarier than it actually is. This section of the test involves you driving for approximately 20 minutes "independently".

Since December 4th 2017, Sat Navs are used in 4 out of 5 tests. The other 1 out of 5 will follow signs or directions given to them by the examiner. You will be able to ask the examiner for confirmation about which way you are supposed to go if you are not sure. This will not get you a fault. Here are some faults that may trip you up during this section of the test:

95. Staring at the Sat Nav

Using the Sat Nav requires you to look at it every now and again to see where you are going and this is highly recommended. There is a problem however if you stare at the Sat Nave for so long that you are not paying attention to the road. This can have serious consequences including losing control of the car.

How to avoid this fault:

- *take glimpses of the sat nav*
- *treat it the same way as you would a mirror*
- *If you are not sure where the sat nav is telling you to go, ask the examiner.*
- *Even if you are a little bit unsure ask the examiner.*

96. Turning last minute

As you go through the independent drive, you might realise really late that you were supposed to turn somewhere. If this happens, DO NOT TURN. It will be better to keep going. You will not fail for missing turns unless that causes other issues. Turning last minute may cause confusion for other road users as they may not be aware that you intend to turn.

How to avoid this fault:

- *plan ahead*
- *If using a Sat Nav, glance at it occasionally as this will show you where the turn is.*
- *If you are not sure where you are supposed to turn, ask the examiner.*
- *Look out for openings in the road, like a large gap between houses*
- *Get used to how far 100, 200, 300 yards is as the sat nav will tell you how far you have until a turn in yards.*
- *If you realise late where the turn is, keep going straight if it is safe to do so.*

Emergency stop

A controlled stop, as it is sometimes referred to will be carried out on some tests. It is not a manoeuvre as such so even if you do one of the four reverse manoeuvres you might still be asked to perform an emergency stop. It is relatively simple to complete but here are some of the ways it can also go wrong:

97. Pressing the clutch before the break

Pressing the clutch before the brake when doing a controlled stop is dangerous for a few of reasons:

- It will reduce the braking effect of the engine
- The time you pressed the clutch could have been used to press the brake
- Your car will travel further before it stops.

Can you think of any more effects pressing the clutch before the brake when doing a controlled stop might have? What could be the consequences of those effects?

How to avoid this fault:

- *Press the brake before the clutch.*
- *If you have an issue with coasting, it is more likely you will make this fault so try to rectify the coasting issue.*

98. Using the handbrake to stop the car

Quite a lot of people seem to think that the handbrake is the best thing to use to stop the car in an emergency. This is not correct. The handbrake is used after you have stopped the car with the footbrake. One of the dangers of using the handbrake instead of the brake is that drivers behind you will not get a warning that you are about to stop as the handbrake does not turn on the brake lights. Can you think of any other reasons why the handbrake should not be used to stop the car?

How to avoid this fault:

- *Practice the emergency stop a few times.*
- *Remember your routine before you drive off just before the emergency stop.*
- *Don't reach for the handbrake straight away as you stop, allow the car to stop first.*

99. Not looking around before moving off after completing the emergency stop

Doing an emergency stop can be quite exciting. In the excitement it can be easy to forget that you have to look around before moving off. You must carry out a full 360 degree check including blind spots before moving your car. Bearing in mind that when you stop you will be in the middle of the road, can you think what might happen if you don't look around before moving off?

How to avoid this fault:

- *Don't rush to move after you have stopped*
- *Take a breath and relax for 3 seconds*
- *Be calm before trying to move off*
- *If there are vehicles trying to go round you before you move off then wait*

End of the test

Believe it or not, most test fails are near the end of the test. It is down to a few things:

- being too relaxed
- losing focus
- thinking that you have passed the test already.

100. Not stopping the car properly when finishing the test

In a lot of test centres, the test will finish in the test centre car park and you may be asked to park the car facing a fence/wall. It is not a manoeuvre but of course you will be expected to stop the car before you get too close to the fence/wall. Sometimes learners forget to brake, yes you read it right, they forget to brake and the examiner has to brake for them to prevent them crashing into the fence.

This fault is becoming less common since most learners will have practiced driving forward into a parking bay as they prepare for their driving test.

How to avoid this fault:

- *drive in very slowly*
- *Know where you are going to stop and start to brake early rather than late.*
- *Press the clutch down early to stop the car going too far forward.*

If you have managed to avoid these faults then you stand a strong chance of passing the test. Nothing beats practicing on the road and getting real experience. Whether you are learning with an instructor, a parent or friend, get out there and experience the road.

I would like to thank you for taking the time to read this book. I want to wish you the best of luck with your driving. For more helpful tips, check out the useful links.

Useful links

www.gozondo.co.uk/blog

Theory test practice

Official DVSA Theory Test Practice Kit

Written by Mark Zondo

Edited by Sydni Okebu

Printed in Great Britain
by Amazon

41656690R00047